The Common Life

THE COMMON LIFE

The Origins of Trinitarian Mysticism
and its Development by Jan Ruusbroec

by Louis Dupré

CROSSROAD · NEW YORK

1984
The Crossroad Publishing Company
370 Lexington Avenue, New York, N.Y. 10017

Copyright © 1984 by Louis Dupré
All rights reserved. No part of this book may be reproduced, stored in a retrieval system, or transmitted, in any form or by any means, electronic, mechanical, photocopying, recording or otherwise, without the written permission of The Crossroad Publishing Company.
Printed in the United States of America

Library of Congress Cataloging in Publication Data
Dupré, Louis K.
The common life.
"Edited text of five lectures I delivered at Gethsemani Abbey, Kentucky, in 1982"—Pref.
1. Trinity—History of doctrines—Middle Ages, 600–1500—Addresses, essays, lectures. 2. Spiritual life—History of doctrines—Middle Ages, 600–1500—Addresses, essays, lectures. 3. Jan, van Ruysbroeck, 1293–1381—Addresses, essays, lectures. I. Title.
BT109.D87   1984   248.2'2   83-23934
ISBN 0-8245-0627-8

Contents

Preface 7

1. The Soul, Image Through Identity 9

2. From Silence to Speech 20

3. From Unity to Trinity 29

4. Rest and Work 38

5. From Trinity to Unity 52

Appendix / *The Spiritual Marriage* 65

Preface

The following pages contain the edited text of five lectures I delivered at Gethsemani Abbey, Kentucky, in 1982. I hesitated long before allowing them to be published and even now I retain some misgivings about my decision. Never have I felt to be dealing with a subject that so totally surpasses my ability to do even minimal justice to it. The final two chapters, in particular, should be read not as a methodic exposé of insights long acquired, but as a reflection of my own, often frustrating attempt to gain access to an ever-alluring yet never-familiar world. The argument that eventually persuaded me to release this tentative sketch lies in the overriding significance of the subject itself. The place of the Trinity in Christian spiritual life demands to be treated, even if it has to be done imperfectly.

Rather than keeping the discussion in general terms I have preferred to turn to a spiritual writer who based his entire theology on the mystery of the Trinity. Yet though the last three chapters focus on Ruusbroec's *The Spiritual Marriage*, they can lay no claim to original scholarship.

I have shamelessly exploited the excellent work done by present members of the Antwerp-based Ruusbroecgenootschap; especially by Albert Ampe, Joseph Alaerts, and Paul Mommaers. Unfortunately most of their work is highly technical and virtually none of it has crossed the ocean. Dom Wijnschenck's old translation, of which I have included excerpts in the appendix, suffers from serious defects, but it remains the one most readily available in America. Soon the Classics of Western Spirituality will bring out an improved translation. To allow the reader to compare the new with the old I have referred to *The Spiritual Marriage* by book and chapter rather than by page number.

I thank the monks of Gethsemani Abbey to have challenged me to this presumptuous but, to me, enriching deed, and Susan Lucibelli, for the patience and ingenuity with which she reconstructed an almost unreadable manuscript into an intelligible text.

·1·
The Soul, Image Through Identity

It is amazing how small a role the Trinity plays in contemporary Christian piety. Both in practical and in spiritual life Christians tend to be pure monotheists. The German theologian Karl Rahner has written that if the dogma of the Trinity were to disappear, the major part of our religious literature could remain unchanged. Even with respect to the Incarnation, Christians rarely realize the significance of the identity of the divine Persons. It happens to be the Son who became flesh. But this theological distinctiveness plays no role in popular piety. The same attitude prevails with respect to that "grace" which, according to our own beliefs, introduces us into the inner life of the Blessed Trinity. We mostly treat it as if it were a created "gift" from God, independent of that personal, triune *presence* which this gift reflects. Such a neglect has not always distorted theology, and until today it has rarely affected the Eastern Church.

For the Greeks "God" does not mean God in general or the three Persons together: God, *Theos*, refers to the Father. This way of speaking agrees with the New Testament. To Jesus, also, God meant the Father. The Synoptic Gospels emphasize the relation between Jesus and his Father, while the Fourth Gospel refers to the Christ as the Word and to his Spirit as the Paraclete. The differences are pronounced, but they (and the Epistles) agree in that little is said about God in an undifferentiated sense.

Let me remind you of a few significant passages. "In the beginning was the Word and the Word was with God and the Word was God. He was in the beginning with God." These words of the Prologue of the Fourth Gospel have become almost meaningless to our own rationalist way of thinking, which owes more to the Deism of the Enlightenment than to the theology of the New Testament. Similarly the beginning of the Epistle to the Hebrews proclaims that God has spoken to us in many ways, through his prophets and last of all through his Son. Introducing the whole creation, the beginning of the Epistle to the Colossians refers to Christ as the Image of the Invisible God, the firstborn, in whom all things were created.

Considering the attitude of the Greek fathers to this scriptural patrimony, we cannot but notice that it differs considerably from the Latin tradition. The Greeks conceived of the ascent to God as taking place in the Logos through the Spirit. We in the Latin world begin with a theory of the one God and add the "distinctions" later. But by that time they no longer relate to the primary object of spiritual theology, man's approach to God. The Greeks, on the contrary, begin directly with the order of salvation. God is the one who has saved us in Christ through the Spirit. The Trinity here appears at the outset, as it does in the New Testament. The Greeks assume that the mode of our knowledge of God, namely, through a revelation in Christ, signifies something about God himself. It is not the revelation *in abstracto* that forms the basis of theological reflection, but the fact that it reached us through the Word, God's personal revelation. This different starting point determines the entire conception of God himself. For it teaches us from the outset that God, rather than being simply one, is the revealing one as well as the revealed. Thus for the Greeks up to our own day, the manifestation, the order of salvation of this "economic" Trinity reveals the nature of the "theological" Trinity. We in the West have not become fully aware of the nature of revelation. In it God does not hand us the crumbs of his table, but manifests his innermost being. Grace is not in the first place a created "gift" added to nature, but the gracious presence of God's self-communicating Word through the Spirit. God is present to us in his own uncreated, internally related being, and this uncreated presence results in a created state of grace.

Let us consider this inner life of God and his revelation of it to us as the Greek fathers describe it. St. Athanasius' approach is most instructive. His *On the Incarnation* does not start from a "dogma" of the Trinity; rather the theological dogma itself results from the *spiritual experience* of the Christian's life in the Church.

This is a fact worthy of reflection, since it was Athanasius who was responsible for articulating the dogmatic structure of the Trinity as we know it today. How far his meditation remains from the kind of higher mathematics we all too readily associate with the trinitarian dogma!

> United to a creature, man would not have been once again deified, if the Son were not true God. Man would not have approached the Father, if He who took on the body had not been the natural and veritable Logos. And just as we would not have been delivered from sin and from malediction if the flesh taken on by the Logos had not been a human flesh by nature....[1]

And again about the Holy Spirit:

> For it is by the Spirit that we are all said to participate in God.... If by the participation of the Spirit we become participants in the divine nature, then it would be foolish to say that the Spirit is of a created nature and not of a divine nature.[2]

The Spirit *must* be God because the Spirit introduces us into the divine life, not the other way around. Note the difference. We Westerners start with one God and virtually dismiss the Trinity as a "mystery" beyond comprehension. This is particularly the case in our own day. I remember hearing at the beginning of a sermon on Trinity Sunday: "The mystery of the Trinity doesn't

---

1. P.G., XXVI, 296 AB.
2. P.G., XXXVI, 588 A.

mean much anymore to people in our age." But if that mystery has lost its meaning, then *what* in Christianity has preserved meaning?

Precisely *because* of this mystery the whole theology of the Greek fathers is mystical through and through. Their interpretation of the scriptural text that man is the image of God, for instance, does not mean that man "appears" somewhat like God, in attitude or task or psychic structure, as some of the Western fathers have presented it. No, the Greek claim expresses a mystical insight unrelated to any external resemblance. It refers to the indwelling of God's uncreated Image in the soul, which makes man himself into a divine image of God. Why is the soul the image of God? Origen answers: Precisely because in it resides the Word, the Logos, which itself is the divine image of God. Rather than starting with difference as we mostly do, the Greek theory of the image starts with the *identity* of the image and that of which it is an image. Whatever extrinsic "resemblance" the soul may bear beyond the presence of the Word itself is no more than the reflection, the external radiation, of that primordial identity. Nor is this identity through the Image the privilege of the saint. It is ontologically inherent in human nature itself. Even the sinner remains in a real sense an image of God, because he continues to host that divine Image, whether he knows it or not. Thus the ascent of spiritual life consists in what Ruusbroec calls a "living toward the Image," that is, in an increasing awareness of, and growing toward, that divine Image which holds the center of my very self. To be created is to exist archetypically in that divine Image of the

Father. But only the mind of a spiritual creature is able to *reflect* this image in its own way, and only the saint, the man or woman of grace, can let it fully shine. Hence to be the image of God means more than "to rule over creation." It refers to the presence of the eternal Word, the reflection of the Father—*lumen de lumine*—light from light. Only the mind can be privileged with this presence, because only the mind can be the habitat, the locus, of the Word. At the same time, the mind can be true to itself only insofar as it brings to full awareness this presence of the Word in itself. For the Christian, spiritual life starts with the conscious presence of the Word, the Image of the Father. Through that Image the mind moves to what the Image reflects and in what it participates, the Father's own divine life.

According to Clement of Alexandria, only the divine *gnosis* introduces us to that awareness of God's presence. *Gnosis* is a somewhat misleading term, because it could imply that study and recollection suffice to unite the soul with God. But this is obviously not what Clement has in mind. He rather means that we are united to God through the full *awareness* of Christ's *presence* in the soul. Christ, then, is the key to that divine *gnosis*: He conveys the outpouring of the Spirit necessary to attain it. In his revelation Christ grants all that is needed for the sacred knowledge of God's inhabitation and of our participation in his nature. Through mystical reflection upon the revelation (*gnosis*), man becomes transformed into what he seeks: like becomes like. To know God, then, is to possess him; to be one with him in knowledge means to be united with him in reality. In the awareness of identity my entire conscious existence comes to partake of the divine unity. Such a *gnosis*, however, is not a matter of study, but of a loving relation to the Logos.

Origen describes the presence of the Word to the soul as that of the spouse who activates the sight, the hearing, the touch, the taste, each sense in accord with its own nature and basic need.

> The eye in beholding the glory of the Son of God would see no other thing nor the ear attend any sound except this living Word. One who touches the living Word will touch henceforth nothing fleeting and mortal. Nor will one's taste, once it has savored the living Word [his flesh, the bread descended from heaven], suffer thereafter the taste of anything else. After this sweetness, all else seems bitterness.... One who has deserved to be thus with Christ tastes and touches the exultant happiness of the Lord. All his senses have their joy in the Word of God.[3]

But the great spiritual theologian of the image of God is the fourth-century Cappadocian Gregory of Nyssa. For him, also, this union with the Word is one of love, of asceticism, of purification, and it is expressed constantly in terms of love. He who is raised in true contemplation to the unity of the divine Image within himself becomes, in fact, united with the Father. Man is capable of seeing God, of being united to God, because he *is* essentially an image of God. Once again, this image is not an external copy of an original reality. It is an image

3. *Commentary on the Song of Songs* I, 4.

only *because*, at some point, it coincides with the original. If the creature resembles God at all, it is because of the initial identity of all creation and especially of the mind with God. The deified mind, then, is the mind that has become fully aware of its divine origin. To be an image for it never means to be an external resemblance, but to reflect externally what it possesses in its deepest ground. Man is capable of seeing God and resembling God because he is already united with God. More than Origen or Clement, St. Gregory of Nyssa emphasizes that this growing toward the Image results in the *love* of God. In the course of its spiritual journey the soul abandons itself to the divine beauty and thus awakens to the divine love. The God whom she encounters in her union with the Word is the Father, not a God beyond the Trinity.

It would, of course, be absurd to claim that Western spiritual theology has ignored the Trinity. The idea of the Trinity appears right from the beginning: Tertullian already uses the term *trinitas*. St. Hilary wrote the first treatise, *De Trinitate*. But the real question is, what the idea, so obviously present from the beginning of Western theology, has *meant* to spiritual life. While in the East the three Persons operate at once upon the soul, each one in a different mode, in the West God's operation in the soul appears as a single effect. All *we* know is one God. There is no *experience* of the distinctions he reveals about himself, nor is there any vital interest in them. This is not to say that the Trinity remains a purely abstract concept. St. Augustine, who is responsible for much of the later speculation, is deeply concerned with finding "images" of the Trinity in human experience.

But these images remain *external* analogies. For him the human mind is an image of the triune God insofar as it consists of three elements, which he, at one point, identified as memory, intellect, and will. To the Greeks such a concept of the image would have appeared inadequate: not an external, mathematical resemblance, but a *distinct presence* renders the soul an image of God. Nevertheless, Augustine's view remains interesting in another respect. For he draws attention to the spiritual impact the presence of the triune God has left upon the soul. The argument here goes from the effect to the cause: the divine presence must have left a trace of the Trinity in the soul itself.

With Augustine the whole spiritual development of Western Christianity took a psychological turn. He was so exclusively introspective during the period immediately following his conversion that his meditations can barely be called specifically Christian. So much seems to be mere reflection, perfectly orthodox, but not very instructive about the specific quality of Christian life. In the *Confessions* he definitively moves *beyond* the self toward a theological introspection. More and more during his final years, Augustine begins with God and seeks the divinelike quality of the soul. The union with God now becomes the starting point. Direct contact of the soul with the Trinity must somehow be reflected in the quality of the soul itself, he assumes. But since he does not have the Greek "economy of salvation" at his disposal, he struggles mightily for clarity in what continues to appear to him a very arcane matter. He clearly overcomes the psychology of his early years. But his psychological orientation remains. Beyond the self we will see the soul, not in its own appearance, but in its divine reality. Here then a direct contact with God will reveal the divine impression upon the soul. Clearly this is not the radically trinitarian approach of the Greeks, but it contains a psychological dimension that is absent in Greek spiritual theology: the mind is able to move beyond itself and thus beyond all psychology, to attain a direct union with God. It is in the *exercise* itself, in the very process of actualizing the trinitarian image in the soul that the union with God occurs. The more we know God, Augustine claims, the more we love him and the more we will be like him. In actualizing the self's own trinity of loving, understanding, and unity, the self becomes ever more united to God and transformed into an image of God. For Augustine the mind's triune quality is a divine image, not because it remembers, understands, and loves itself (that is a merely external resemblance), but because it has the power to remember, to understand, and to love *its Origin*. This means, if I understand Augustine correctly, that the soul is an image of the divine Trinity only *because* it is already united with the Trinity. The mind is able to remember God (the *memoria Dei*), to understand and to love him and thereby transforms the external image of the Trinity in the soul, into a real, intrinsic image. At this point Augustine comes close to the Greek idea that the image is grounded in an identity. For the Greeks the theology of the image of God, above all, asserted the soul's initial, fundamental *identity* with God. St. Augustine's approach is different. He does not *start* from the soul's initial identity, but from its threefold function which bears the imprint of the Trinity. This is an external resemblance until, through remembrance, understanding, and love, the soul is drawn into God's own life and thereby becomes an ontological image of God.

Unfortunately Augustine's basic identity was soon forgotten and only the superficial resemblance retained. We shall have to wait for the Cistercians (especially William of St. Thierry), the Victorines, and, later, Ruusbroec to discover the more profound insight that man is an image of God because in his deepest essence he is identical with God—with the Father, through the Son, in the Holy Spirit.

·2·

From Silence to Speech

For the Greek Church fathers, the Blessed Trinity has always stood in the center of spiritual life. No abstract, purely theoretical idea of one God preceded the Trinity. The economy of salvation, that is, the order of redemption, determined all theology: from the Word to the Father in the Spirit. In contrast to this radically theological approach, the Western fathers stayed close to immediate experience. Since God stands entirely beyond that experience, he becomes an asymptotic point of unity to which experience points without ever attaining it. The Trinity is exclusively a matter of revelation. Nevertheless, Augustine and the few who later followed him reached, in a different way, a richer idea of experience. Once the soul begins to recognize in itself a fundamental unity with the revealed being of God, the external analogies of the soul with the Trinity (such as the three functions in one mind) take on a deeper, mystical meaning. Awakened to God's *presence* in itself, the soul becomes alert to the traces and reflections of that mysterious inhabitation.

it, but he is in it, for the Father begets his Son in the soul exactly as he does in eternity and not otherwise. He must do so whether he will or not. The Father ceaselessly begets his Son. And what is more, he begets me as his Son— the self-same Son."[2] In these daring words Eckhart states that the divine self-expression in the Word contains all other expressions. Since the Son is the firstborn of all creatures (Col. 1:15), all creatures, particularly the spiritual ones, retain their primordial being in that divine Image of God. Eckhart here follows the theology of the Greek fathers. But he radicalizes it in stating that in its innermost being, at that point where it touches God's creative act, the soul coincides with the divine Image. In its uncreated core the soul never leaves the eternal immanence of the Son in the Father. Because of that primordial immanence the soul is called to turn its whole being toward that divine Image. To do so it must, as much as possible, become what it already is in its uncreated core and leave all creatures and, eventually, all created distinctions behind. In comparison to that divine core creatures possess no reality. Not only are they not important, but in Eckhart's conception they have no part in the soul's final destiny.

How, then, can I become *Godlike*? How can I be both a created image of God and coincide at some point with God's uncreated Image? For Eckhart this is a concrete and vital issue. In a sermon that begins with the words "Like a vase of gold," Eckhart explains that every image has two properties. First, it participates in that of which

---

2. *Meister Eckhart: A Modern Translation* by Raymond Bernard Blakney (New York: Harper Torchbook, 1957), p. 181.

it is an image. But next, being *only* an image, it is distinct from the original. When looking at a portrait you exclaim, "That is really him," you emphasize the identity—this *is* the same person. But you may also conclude, "Well, that is not a bad likeness," and then you indicate that the image differs from the original. An image is a dynamic reality that constantly moves from difference to identity and back. Eckhart perceived, as the Greek fathers had done, that to call man an image is to assert that in his deepest being he is already united with God, but also that the whole purpose of spiritual life is to move toward a more complete union. What could that mean but to overcome, as much as possible, that part of myself which is only an external likeness? Its goal then is to overcome not only the dissimilarity but also the similarity in order to move toward identity. Whatever is only "like" God, because it bears the imprint of his creative act, must, as much as possible, be converted to identity. Image theology must become theology of identity and gradually abandon all likeness, image, and metaphor. We cannot assert anything positive about God, not even that He *is*, for if creation *is*, God is not. Even to attribute to God the almost empty predicate of *oneness* is too much. The One is still a creaturely manifestation of the divine reality which fails to express God's "reality." In the end nothing remains but the barren Godhead of which the Trinity itself is only a revelation to the creature. The soul moving toward identity with God moves in fact toward a state in which no more activity or form exist.

Does Eckhart simply mean that, at some point, in

growing toward the Image the soul ends up in darkness, because with the Son she has moved into the dark desert of the Father? Or does he mean that the created mind in its spiritual ascent moves into a divine reality where the distinctions between Father, Son, and Holy Spirit no longer exist? The latter position is highly controversial from a spiritual as well as from a theological viewpoint, and if Eckhart held it, the bishop of Cologne was right to attack it. A passage such as the following raises questions about the interpretation of his theology. "If God is to steal into it [the little castle in the soul], it [the adventure] will cost Him all his divine names and personlike properties; He would have to forgo all these if he is to gain entrance. Except as He is the onefold One, without ways or properties—neither the Father nor the Holy Spirit in the [personal] sense, yet something that is neither this nor that—see!—it is only as He is One and onefold that He may enter into that One which I have called the Little Castle."[3] Is it true that in the Godhead there is only silence, "because there is nothing to talk about"?[4] Or is he merely asserting that in the mystical darkness the soul realizes that even the highest symbols of revelation are still phrased in human language and, hence, do not express God's full reality?

The question may appear somewhat specious and void of spiritual significance. But whether there is a continuing internal dynamism at work in God or whether the divine expression in the Word and in Creation ultimately comes to rest in total silence is a highly practical problem

3. Ibid., p. 211.
4. Ibid., p. 225.

in spiritual life. When we grow toward the Image and allow God's immanence to penetrate ever more of our being, we have to shed our attachment to creation and to enter into total darkness and silence. For that reason Eckhart's silence appeals to all who are seriously engaged upon a spiritual life. Those who enjoy the closest familiarity with God are most reluctant to be loose-lipped about him. But sooner or later the question arises: How can we continue to use words at that point? Is silence the end? Is a purely negative theology itself not a "creaturely" approach to God? Should it not, at some point, abandon also its own creaturely reservations and in the absence of words of its own listen to the Word that God himself has spoken? After all, the God with whom I am united *manifests* himself through his own revelation in the Son. Hence should we not say that in God's silence I hear the Word, in his darkness I see the Light, in his rest I enjoy his active Love?

No one has described this internal dynamism within God more articulately than Jan Ruusbroec. In the Western tradition he most fully understood the spiritual meaning of the mystery of the Trinity. Ruusbroec also knew that darkness without light, that silence in which there are no more words. But he never considered them the end of all spiritual life. For the realm of silence and darkness *is* the Father, that is, a silence that expresses itself in the eternal self-manifestation of the Word, a darkness in which the Light originates. Ruusbroec invites us to follow the Father's generation of the Son and the return of the Son to the Father. Unceasingly, we move into the darkness, abandon distinctions, and then move out again in the revelation of the Word. From God's rest to God's works and back into the rest, in a never-ending ebb and flow.

Eckhart's theology went astray when it placed the Absolute *beyond* the Trinity, the Godhead *beyond* the Father. Had the darkness and silence into which the soul moves been identified with the Father, then she would have been able to go out again into speech and into light. The Father is, indeed, the principle of darkness and silence, but a darkness that is to break out into Light, a silence that is to speak the Word. The theology of the Image leads to what lies beyond images. Negative theology is an essential part of it. But it is not the final way station on the soul's spiritual pilgrimage. Even Eckhart's own disciple, John Tauler, knew this. In his twenty-ninth sermon he shows how the Trinity inhabits the soul. "We should learn to find the Trinity in ourselves and realize we are in a *real* way formed according to its image."[5] Note the word *"real"*: it refers to a partial identity. Even in its natural state the soul, however imperfect, bears this divine image. Being a finite reflection of that perfect Image of God's self-expression, the soul participates in the divine life of the Son. Spiritual progress consists "in recognizing this blessed image in ourselves above all things."[6] This core in which I am most myself is, as Augustine taught, God's presence in me. "It is impossible to describe adequately the nobility of this image, for God is in this image, and indeed is the image, while

---

5. John Tauler, *Spiritual Conferences*, trans. and edited by Eric Colledge and Sister M. Jane, O.P. (Rockford, Ill.: Tan Books, 1961), p. 141.
6. Ibid.

yet being imageless."⁷ And yet there is also a clear dissimilarity, an element of insurmountable difference. The very *similarity* indicates a shortcoming of the image and, hence, the presence also of dissimilarity. The soul ought to move beyond likeness and similarity toward that point where equality and inequality coincide. In this divine abyss the soul loses itself and knows nothing of God or of itself, of likeness to him or of difference from him. In the identity the soul loses all sense of distinctions. Hence, Tauler informs us in the sixth sermon, anyone formed in this image of God will find all other images dim and worthless, including the so-called images of God. The real image is my identity with God, my being in the Son. "Once men are free of images, the divine sun shines into them and they are most marvelously drawn out of themselves and out of all earthly things."⁸ Hence the real image of God in me consists of my super-essential being within the divine reality, that part of my being where God touches me in his creative activity. Spiritual life moves toward that point of identity. The movement of identification, never complete, results in darkness and silence as the expression returns to what it expresses. Yet darkness and silence are not final. For the God we reach has spoken and continues to speak his eternal Word. Only in the divine silence can we clearly hear God's Word, in the divine night see God's Light. About this Word in silence, this Light in the night, Ruusbroec wrote.

7. Ibid.
8. Ibid., p. 128.

·3·

From Unity to Trinity

A little over six hundred years ago the Blessed Jan Ruusbroec, Western Christianity's most articulate interpreter of the trinitarian mystical tradition, died. He lived during a period of unabated physical and social calamities: the Hundred Years War, the Black Plague, the Avignon exile. But the same fourteenth century also produced an unparalleled upsurge of spiritual life stirred by such great mystics as Eckhart, Suso, Tauler, Catherine of Siena, Birgitta of Vadstena, Richard Rolle, Walter Hilton, and the author of the *Cloud of Unknowing*.

In some unique way, Ruusbroec synthesizes Eastern and Western spirituality. In the East spiritual knowledge related to the specific identities of the Father, the Son, and the Holy Ghost in the works of creation as well as in those of salvation. The West, taking a more psychological approach, tended to direct its aspirations and reflections toward the one God or the God-man often unrelated to the other Persons. Still, as we noted, eventually Augustine's religious psychology developed into a mystical theology of the Trinity. Ruusbroec attained a perfect balance between the psychological and the objective trinitarian approach. For him the soul partakes in the constant flowing out and turning in of the Trinity, the perpetual generation of the Persons and the contraction into the unity of one nature. In the divine Image of the Son, man is called to participate directly in that divine ebbing and flowing. God's creative act is the point in which God and man touch. Since the entire creation pre-exists archetypically in the Son (Colossians), the creature is a partial, finite expression of God's perfect self-expression in the Son. The purpose of spiritual life is precisely to assimilate, as much as possible, our created being, to that uncreated divine Image. Man's destiny is "deification," as the Greek fathers so daringly claimed, or, as Ruusbroec expresses it, growing toward the divine Image.

Unlike Eckhart, Ruusbroec places an equal emphasis on God's unity and Trinity. For him the ascending movement toward divine unity does not conclude spiritual life. God is ebbing and flowing: after having moved into unity the Trinity expresses itself in the distinctness of Persons and, within that expression, of the entire creation. Ruusbroec firmly rejects the theory (which appears to enjoy a revival in spiritual movements today) according to which God's being is total darkness, absolute oneness, into which everything comes to a definitive rest. True, there is a moment of unity without distinctions, but for Ruusbroec spiritual life constantly moves beyond this static point. Those who refuse to follow this movement beyond unity, he claims, merely want to rest in themselves. Ruusbroec persistently polemicized against this kind of unitarian mysticism. "When a man is bare and imageless in his senses, and empty and idle in his higher powers, he enters into rest through mere nature" (II, 66). Spiritual exercises may, by sheer human effort, create silence and rest, perfectly legitimate qualities in their own right. But God's life knows no rest. It urges man to move out again. The point here is not that the spiritual person should seek contemplation and then convey its fruits to others—*contemplata tradere*. For Ruusbroec true *contemplation* itself demands that we move out of the divine rest, but that we do so with the divine Persons. If the Christian allows grace to operate freely within him, grace will urge him on to "works." The experience of rest is not, and never was, the ideal of Christian contemplation. Grace moves the soul to partake in God's own flowing and ebbing, back and forth. "This flowing of God demands always a flowing back; for God is a sea that ebbs and flows, pouring without ceasing into all his beloved according to the need and the merits of each, and ebbing back again with all those who have been thus endowed in heaven and earth with all that they have and all that they can" (II, 40). Spiritual life is a cycle, not a finite line.

What Ruusbroec denounces with a touch of irony as a purely natural state of rest—remaining quiet, without either outward or inward acts, untroubled by any cares —many today consider the ideal of contemplation. The state of rest sought as an end in itself, forgetful of God and blind to our neighbor's care, falls far short of the Christian ideal.

> It is a sitting still, without either outward or inward acts, in vacancy, in order that rest may be found and may remain untroubled. But a rest which is practiced in this way is unlawful, for it brings with it in men a blindness and ignorance and a sinking down into themselves without activity. Such a rest is nought else than an idleness into which the man has fallen and in which he forgets himself and God and all things in all that has to do with activity.... And in this natural rest one cannot find God but it certainly leads a man into a bare vacancy, which may be found by Pagans and Jews and all men—how wicked soever they may be, if they can live in their sins without reproach of their conscience and can empty themselves of every image and of all activity. (Ibid.)

Clearly Ruusbroec rejects the state of quiet as the end of spiritual life. The exclusive pursuit of rest betrays a desire to stay within one's psychic limits and obstructs God's *own* operation.

For Ruusbroec the *unity* of divine life is not beyond the Trinity, as Eckhart taught, but is rather the initial moment of the trinitarian cycle. It corresponds to Gregory of Nyssa's dark cloud which we enter, but in which we find the light. In *The Spiritual Marriage* Ruusbroec distinguishes the superessential unity of God, in which Father and Son possess their nature in the unity of the Holy Ghost, from the moment of Trinity in which the divine Persons relate to one another. In this divine unity God dwells above all distinctions in his uncreated light. But this unity of the divine nature breaks out into the fertility of the Father who unceasingly generates his

From St. Gregory of Nyssa we learned that the soul's ascent toward its archetypal Image does not consist merely in an increase in cognition but, above all, in a growing in love. Yet that love itself creates its own spiritual enlightenment. In his commentary on the Song of Songs, St. Gregory describes the stages of this enlightenment. Initially the conversion to the Image is marked by a transition from darkness to light. But as the soul penetrates more deeply into the divine realm, the light grows dimmer. A cloud overshadows the world of appearances. In the end the soul, having left behind all that pertains to human nature, enters within the secret chamber of the divine knowledge. Here darkness surrounds her on all sides, and beyond sense and reason she remains aware only of the invisible and the incomprehensible presence. Even as Moses entered into the dark cloud wherein God dwelled, the soul at the end of her spiritual journey encounters only darkness. Significantly, the very theologians who have most deeply explored the inner recesses of God's presence to the soul are the ones who most firmly assert our inability to grasp that presence in human cognition.

Similar descriptions of the development from light to darkness appear in the West once the Cistercians rediscover the Greek fathers. The process from the Son to the Father leads not into light but into darkness. In ascending to the Image, according to William of St. Thierry, we have to leave behind all images that are not *like* God. Since no creature is "like God," this in the end becomes an appeal to abandon the created realm altogether. Like the Greek fathers, William in *The Golden*

Epistle distinguishes the animal level and the level of reason from that of spirit, where contemplation takes place. "When the object of thought is God, and the will reaches the state at which it becomes love, the Holy Spirit at once infuses himself by way of love.... The understanding of the one thinking becomes the contemplation of one loving."[1] The presence of God through the Son in the Holy Spirit manifests itself as infused love and knowledge combined. *Contemplatio est amor.* William insistently warns the spiritual novice against the temptation of comparing the divine reality with human appearances. In thinking of its likeness to God, the soul must first mold its thought so as to avoid conceiving of God in representations. Indeed, the closer the soul moves toward the Image of God that is in its deepest self, the more it must leave behind all external images.

The dialectical tension between divine Image and created likeness culminates in the writings of Meister Eckhart. By his time the trinitarian spiritual theology, first formulated by the Greeks and propagated in the West by the Cistercians and by the Benedictines of St. Victor Abbey in Paris, had become widely accepted. We clearly notice its influence on Eckhart's own thought. In one of the German sermons he writes: "In eternity the Father begets the Son in his own likeness. 'The Word was with God and the Word was God.' Like God, it had his nature. Furthermore, I say that God has begotten him in my soul. Not only is the soul like him and he like

---

1. *The Golden Epistle*, trans. Theodore Berkeley (Kalamazoo: Cistercian Publications, 1980), nos. 249–50.

eternal Word. This Word, through the Spirit, rejoins the aboriginal unity. The Father knows the Son and in the Son all things, and the Son knows the Father and all things in the Father, for they are one simple nature.

In the act of creation God touches my own being, regardless of my state of perfection, whether I be a saint or a sinner. God is *naturally* present to the soul, at the point where his creating act results in my created being. In confessing that God has created me, I affirm that, at some point, his act and my being coincide. That is the basis upon which the spiritual theology of grace rests, the heart of *Christian* mysticism.

In *The Spiritual Marriage*, Ruusbroec describes the spiritual process in three stages. Following the Cistercians (especially William of St. Thierry), Ruusbroec distinguishes three kinds of human powers: the lower ones of the sensuous life; the higher powers of intellect, memory, and will; and, beyond this ordinary consciousness, the powers of the *spirit*.

Each of these powers strives toward simplicity. Thus, sensuous activity becomes recollected in the unity of the heart, the unifying organ that coordinates all lower activities. In Ruusbroec's theology this is the sphere of virtue, of the moral life. In the second sphere, to which he refers as the inner life, occurs the unification of the higher powers of the mind—of intellect, memory, and will. Their goal also is to achieve the greatest possible unity. The soul here already becomes a mystical mirror of the Blessed Trinity. Finally, on the highest level, the level of the spirit, the soul, "beyond all its faculties, beyond all its powers," attains "its naked essence." This essence of the soul consists not in a self-enclosed state, but in an opening to that superessence of God. "Like the prime mover which touches this first sphere of heavens in Aristotle's astronomy, God touches the creature . . . in this superessential unity" (II, 49). That bare essence of our createdness is the natural foundation of all mysticism, the primary link of the creature with God. To realize this union, to develop it as much as possible, is the whole purpose of spiritual life.

The three moments of spiritual life do not succeed each other in a linear diachrony. They keep returning in succession. Thus the cardinal virtues of the moral life are gradually enriched with the passive gifts of the Holy Spirit. In the course of spiritual life, morality itself fundamentally changes from what it was before the spiritual ascent. If a person allows himself to be transformed by divine grace, his moral striving attains another dimension. Virtue becomes transformed by infused virtue. In the second part, Ruusbroec deals with the inner life as such, the union with God achieved by the soul as principle of the higher functions of mind, memory, and will. Ruusbroec describes this process, both active and passive, by means of an exegesis of the cry in the Parable of the Wise and Foolish Virgins: "Behold, the bridegroom comes; go out to meet him!" (Matt. 25:6). For Ruusbroec these words refer to the mystical advent of Christ. Of the traditional three comings, into this world (the Incarnation), into our hearts (through sacraments and prayer), and at the Last Judgment, he only discusses the second.

Ruusbroec distinguishes three ways in which Christ comes into our hearts. The first coming consists in the longing for God. As a form of desire Ruusbroec connects it with the lower, sensuous powers. "The first coming of Christ in inward working drives and urges a man in his inward feeling; it draws him with all his powers upwards to heaven, and it calls him to unite himself with God. This driving and drawing we feel in the heart, and in the unity of all the bodily powers, and especially in the desirous power" (II, 5). In the second coming, Christ enters "with a higher nobleness, more after his likeness" (II, 6) into the higher powers of the soul. Here begins the interior life in which the mind is enlightened and the higher powers become "adorned" with spiritual gifts. In a third way, God moves the soul "by an inward stirring or touch in the unity of the spirit" (II, 7). In this experience of simple presence, the higher powers of the soul are reunited in the spirit from which they flow forth.

To each one of these comings corresponds a special mode of going out to meet Christ. To the first belongs the active practice of a virtuous life. The second coming is received in the recollected attitude proper to the interior of a "God-seeking" life. In the third, mystical coming, the soul withdraws from all multiplicity, from all powers, into pure unity. It unifies not only the sensuous consciousness but also the higher powers of will and intellect. This unification process has an "essential" (*weselijc*) as well as an "active" (*werkelijc*) aspect. Ruusbroec refers to God's direct communication to the soul—without intermediary—as the *essential* unity. Through it the soul partakes in the divine life. But even at the highest level of union where God alone works, the contemplative person must, in union with the distinct Persons of the Trinity, move out again into activity.

The essentially static presentation of spiritual life as occurring in three phases is misleading. The stages do not follow in succession: they imply one another. In the interior life a person must still actively practice virtue and even the contemplative must return to some forms of active life. At the same time, the interior life transcends its own active quality and becomes passive. It eventually leads to the contemplative life. In this constant dialectic between the three forms of spiritual life—the virtuous, the interior, and the contemplative—consists "the common life" (*dat ghemeyne leven*), the specific mode of being and acting that follows the rhythm of the Trinity itself. Through it the soul attains the ultimate goal of its spiritual striving, namely, the highest possible identity with its divine Image.

Our final two chapters will deal with the third coming of Christ. This forms the subject of the third book of *The Spiritual Marriage*. But since the interior life normally results in contemplation, Ruusbroec initiates the discussion in the final chapters of the second book (reprinted at the end of this edition). The theme is announced.

> Through this loving inclination of God and his inward working in the unity of our spirit, . . . there arises the third coming of Christ in inward working. And this is an inward touch or stirring of Christ in His divine brightness, in the inmost part of our spirit. . . . And this grace springs up within the unity of our spirit like a fountain, and falls back again into that same unity whence it arises; even

> as a living and gushing spring which comes forth from the living ground of the divine richness where neither faithfulness nor grace can ever fail. And this is the touch which I mean. And the creature passively endures this touch.... Here no one works save God alone (II, 51).

When God and the soul touch, a constant ebbing and flowing begins, a rising and falling, that follows the rhythm of God's internal life. God acts alone within the unity of the spirit, above the multiplicity of personal effort. Nevertheless, on the first level of this mystical passivity, which we shall consider in the next chapter, the "touch" itself still mediates as a final "intermediary" between God and the creature. What theology has traditionally called "created grace" consists in the created effect caused by God's presence. Eventually the mystical experience surpasses this created grace and directly confronts God's uncreated presence to the soul.

·4·

Rest and Work

Spiritual life for Ruusbroeck consists in a process of gradual unification and simplification. The first stage, the "virtuous life," already achieves some unity through the gifts of the Holy Spirit. Nevertheless, the life of virtue remains mainly an active longing for God through good works. In the second stage the soul, purified and enlightened, becomes unified in the higher faculties of intellect, memory, and will. It gradually prepares itself for the third coming of Christ, the simplest mode of unity. In these final two chapters we shall concentrate on the third stage, first as it is described in the final chapters of the second book of *The Spiritual Marriage*, then in the four chapters of the third book.

I once heard a monk explain the meaning of monastic life. His surprising description may help us to understand what Ruusbroec has in mind. You pass through various stages of happiness and desolation until you reach a point where you think you cannot stand it anymore. Then, if all goes well, there comes a moment when God becomes more important to you than you to yourself. What characterizes this moment are not intensive feelings, or a great display of virtue, but an attitude of total trust. To one who attains that attitude, all of spiritual life begins to make sense. Otherwise is doesn't. It is the message so boldly written above the gate of the Gethsemani guesthouse: "God alone." These two words contain the entire ideal of spiritual life. Monastic life is, after all, no more than an institutional way to overcome the many compromises with the world which inhibit the development of spiritual life. In this third stage Ruusbroec presents the life in which God alone has become important. As we saw in the previous chapter, the life with God at its hightest level can either be "essential" (*weselijc*) or "active" (*werkelijc*). The essential mode of being refers to the presence of God "in the nakedness of its nature, without means and without interruption" (II, 57). In an essential sense the soul has its being in God's eternal Image. Without interruption it receives the impress of the divine Archetype and, like that Image itself, remains a dwelling place of God's presence.

> The spirit in its essence possesses God in the nakedness of its nature, as God does the spirit: for it lives in God and God in it. And it is able, in its highest part, to receive, without intermediary, the Brightness of God, and all that God can fulfill .... and it flows forth again, through the eternal birth of the Son, together with all the other creatures, and is set in its created being by the free will of the Holy Trinity. And here it is like unto the image of the most high Trinity in Unity, in which it has been made. And, in its created being, it incessantly re-

ceives the impress of its Eternal Archetype, like a flawless mirror, in which the image remains steadfast, and in which the reflection is renewed without interruption by its ever-new reception in new light. This essential union of our spirit with God does not exist in itself, but it dwells in God, and it flows forth from God, and it depends upon God, and it returns to God as to its Eternal Origin. (II, 57)

Ruusbroec describes here the divine ground of all createdness, the ontological basis of the mystical life. I have always wondered how women and men muster the courage to choose that most daring mode of existence—the Godlike life. They take seriously what, in spite of all pious claims, few take seriously, and they have little concern for matters which for others are of utmost importance. How, for instance, can a genuinely religious person lead a life that is so much at variance with ordinary human aspirations? In the passage quoted Ruusbroec provides the answer: Because God remains present at the core of my existence and invites me to total union. St. Bernard describes this beloved union in highly erotic language. But even that expression remains inadequate, because lovers are never as close to one another as God is to the soul. The spirit in its *essence* refers to that point of unity where it receives God "in the nakedness of its nature." The expression "without means," that is, without intermediacy, indicates that nothing stands between God and the soul. At the root of my existence, in that primeval Image of my uncreated being, no creature screens me from God. In its "naked nature" the mind bears the imprint of its eternal Archetype, or, more correctly, the soul remains *in* that Archetype.

To be created does not mean that we are on our own after God got things started. We have never left him: In him we continue to live, to move, and to be. Our very existence is the space in which God dwells. Though few may realize this divine presence in the soul, it remains no less real for it. Any concept of man that fails to include this transcendent dimension is flawed. God's own being is the axis around which the self moves. Its superessential unity places the self in God's constant presence. "The spirit, according to its essence, receives the coming of Christ in the nakedness of its nature, without means and without interruption." The birth of the Son is not an event in the past, indeed, not an event at all, but a dynamic process in which each Person of the Trinity remains eternally involved. The whole creation participates in that generating process. Each thought, each word, each act constantly reflects the Father's self-expression in the Son. All partake in God's ceaseless expression in his eternal Word. "For where He comes, there He is; and where He is, there He comes." If God is able to visit the soul, it is because he is already there. It is not simply that he is present in me. I am in him, for he never leaves himself. The Son remains in the Father, and in the Son all things remain as in their Archetype. The mind possesses God "in the nakedness of its nature" only because God possesses the mind. Inseparably, my essence is joined to his essence. Ruusbroec insists that if this nature were to be separated from God, it would vanish into pure nothingness. "This is that nobleness which we possess by nature in the essential unity of our spirit, where it is united with God according to nature. This neither makes us holy nor blessed, for all men, whether good or evil, possess it within themselves" (II, 57). But if the presence is natural, our awareness of it is not. Only the truly spiritual person grows "toward the Image." For we must receive it from God.

Having defined the *essence* of the soul, Ruusbroec next discusses the *works* that correspond to this mystical union. These no longer consist in the pursuit of virtue, although works of virtue remain to the very end an essential part of spiritual life. God himself invites and enables the soul to actualize its habitual union with God. Its response to this call initiates that "supernatural" union which renders a person "like unto God through grace and virtue" (II, 58). This "likeness" of the virtuous person is not given by nature, as the similarities and analogies of which St. Augustine wrote; it results from divine grace and religious response. "Likeness" remains in the created order. But the grace that effects it accompanies the uncreated union with the blessed Trinity. One conditions the other. The spirit that actualizes the union with its divine Archetype becomes "like" it. "Whenever we turn to Him with our whole will . . . at that very moment, Christ comes to us and in us, both with means [i.e., through the intermediacy of grace and virtue] and without means [i.e., through the uncreated union with God], that is, with the virtues and above the virtues. And He impresses His image and His likeness in us, namely Himself and His gifts" (II, 58). Like a flawless mirror, the contemplative reflects God's gracious presence in his soul.

Created grace, in virtue and good works, manifests the uncreated union with the Trinity in the essence of the soul. In this *active* reflection, then, consists the "other mode" in which the spirit maintains that essential unity with God of which Ruusbroec teaches that it "does not exist in itself, but . . . dwells in God" (II, 57). Here the unity functions as a source of power and strength that overflows in a multiplicity of works and virtues. Thus in its own created way the soul both reflects and resembles God's uncreated Image. Though this reflection still remains in the order of "likeness," it presents more than an external resemblance, since it derives directly from the uncreated union which it extends into the created order. As such, it is related to that dynamic "image" of God described by Gregory of Nyssa which, rather than being a "given" entity, consists in the very process of growing toward a fuller identity with God. Nevertheless, the entire created image and likeness remains subordinate, and indeed instrumental, to the uncreated union. Unfortunately most believers never become aware of this uncreated grace. Grace to them is primarily a "gift" that assists them in their practice of virtue and their efforts to lead the good life. The uncreated presence remains hidden and unattended. In fact, created grace with its apparel of virtues and gifts is both the overflow of, and the way to, that union without means. Ruusbroec stresses its instrumental role: "Grace is a God-formed light, which shines through us and makes us like to God: and without this light, which makes us God-like, we cannot be united with God supernaturally, even though we cannot lose the image of God nor our natural unity with Him" (II, 58). It frees the spirit for that supreme meeting and union "without means and above nature . . . wherein our highest blessedness consists" (II, 58).

This union with God, above likeness and means, as Ruusbroec describes it (in chapter 59), takes place in the spirit, "deeply hidden from our understanding." Yet the spirit has its own "essential intuition" (*weselijcken begripe*). "In the fruition of this unity we shall rest evermore, above ourselves and above all things. From this unity, all gifts, both natural and supernatural, flow forth, and yet the loving spirit rests in this unity above all gifts; and here there is nothing but God, and the spirit united with God without means" (II, 59). Ruusbroec uses the language of love throughout *The Spiritual Marriage*. At this highest moment he refers to the "loving spirit" and "the fruition of unity." Still this way of speaking must not be understood as expressing an encounter between two persons. The union takes place in the spirit's "naked essence" and, indeed, gives that spirit its own unity. At the same time, the love language is appropriate insofar as the union is not one between two abstract principles but with the *Persons* of the Trinity. These trinitarian distinctions mark the entire contemplative life. Even at the moment of most intimate unity the distinctness of the Persons does not disappear. God remains triune even where the Persons turn into the unity of their one divine nature—above all divine modes. It is too early to discuss the dialectic between unity and trinity as it involves the contemplative mind. The third book of *The Spiritual Marriage* will introduce this very complex subject. Yet the uncreated union—above means—discussed at the end of the second book deals exclusively with *the Trinity as such*. Whenever Ruusbroec discusses God's unity in this context, he refers to one of the Persons and thus explicitly connects the unity with the Trinity. "In this unity we are taken possession of by the Holy Ghost, and we take possession of the Holy Ghost and the Father and the Son, and the whole Divine Nature: for God cannot be divided" (II, 59).

At the beginning of the essential union, all distinctions disappear from the experience. "The spirit plunges itself and loses itself, as regards the highest part of its life" (II, 57). In its own essential depth, which is God's own depth, the soul begins by experiencing a total waylessness. Once it has let go of creation nothing remains to which it can hold. The ensuing feeling of nothingness corresponds to the concept of emptiness common in the negative theology, but unlike Eckhart, Ruusbroec firmly keeps this pure unity without determination *within* the Trinity. The One is not a God above God, indeed it is not even the "one nature" as distinct from the triune God. The initial impact of God's presence on the spirit is, indeed, silence. But Ruusbroec interprets this silence as "fertile," that is, as ready to break out into speech. As such, it becomes identified with the Father and announces the birth of the Son. Only after the soul has fully participated in the dialogue among the Persons will it discover the concrete unity of God's nature.

Even at this early stage of contemplation, Ruusbroec insists that the soul can enjoy no permanent rest without going out into works and into creation. He does write: "In the fruition of this unity we shall rest evermore, above ourselves and above all things" (II, 59). But surrounding texts make it abundantly clear that "evermore" does not mean rest *without* works, but rather continuing rest in God's unity *even while* the contemplative moves out into the multiplicity of works. Later it will appear how this "outgoing" itself, far more than a continuance of the practice of virtue and good works, consists, in fact, in a direct participation in the circumincessional motion within the Trinity itself. Even here, while stressing the permanence of the contemplative rest, Ruusbroec hints at the motion of work: "[A]nd there [the spirit] *abidingly* possesses its eternal blessedness; and it *flows forth again*, through the eternal birth of the Son, together with all the other creatures, and is set in its created being by the free will of the Holy Trinity" (II, 57). No spiritual rest remains without motion, and no spiritual motion without rest. The two moments of the contemplative life, the ingoing into unity and the outflowing into multiplicity, never appear separately. Having met God on the top of the mountain, the contemplative cannot afford to stay there in idleness. No sooner has Ruusbroec completed his description of the rest in union than he adds a section on the need to "go out towards Him [Christ] through means, that is, through virtues and various practices" (II, 60). Even the perfect contemplative must go out and return to God "through means," that is, through grace, virtue, and devout practice, if he or she is to preserve the uncreated union from relapsing into a residual state of consciousness.

Ruusbroec speaks of a "perpetual renewal" in which

God gives ever-new gifts, and the spirit, in its response, "grows continually into a higher life" (II, 60). Yet the world to which the contemplative returns is not the one he left. It has become completely transformed. In the divine perspective creation emerges, within the Son, from the Father's generating act, in order to return, within the Son, to the Father. This new perspective, far from distorting the view, allows the contemplative to perceive creation as it is in its essence. Only to the spiritual person does creation fully manifest itself. Nature as St. Francis faced it after his conversion had become purer, more beautiful, and indeed, more intensively real. His vision of it changed the entire outlook of his culture and, in some way, still retains its impact today. He had discovered a new dimension to the real. Wherever the life of the spirit is lived, the environment, however sober and sparse, acquires a sudden harmonious completeness: nothing seems to be missing where the essential is present. Creation appears to yield itself only to nonpossessive eyes, ears, and hands.

God's grace accompanies and guides the spirit during its outward journey, so that it may return, enriched and refreshed, to its uncreated union. For Ruusbroec God remains present in my createdness as much as in my uncreated essence, where I separate from him as much as where I am one with him, in likeness as much as beyond likeness. The ceaseless drawing in and flowing out of spiritual life follows the rhythm of God's inner being. In a continuous act the Father gives birth to the Son and, in the Son, to all creation. Then, in the same movement the Son returns to the Father and, in the Son, so does the entire creation. Ruusbroec's articulation of spiritual life incorporates the expanding and contracting rhythm of all life. Indeed it conveys life its ultimate, mystic foundation.

Ruusbroec concludes his treatment of the interior life with a lyrical description of the first stage of the essential union with God in which the God-seeking life results: "Now understand this well: that measureless Splendour of God, which together with the incomprehensible brightness, is the cause of all gifts and of all virtues— that same Uncomprehended Light transfigures the fruitive tendency of our spirit and penetrates it in a way that is wayless; that is, through the Uncomprehended Light. And in this light the spirit immerses itself in fruitive rest; for this rest is wayless and fathomless, and one can know of it in no other way than through itself—that is, through rest" (II, 64). After the triune God has united himself directly with the spirit, all common concepts or distinctions cease to apply. Whatever is to be learned or experienced must directly be revealed by God himself. The soul meets God *through God* rather than through itself. "[U]nited without means, and made one with the Spirit of God, we can meet God through God, and everlastingly possess with Him and in Him our eternal bliss" (II, 64). Thus the ideal of the Godlike life has been attained. God has finally become more important to me than I am to myself: He has taken over my whole essential being. My essence has now come to coincide with my superessence—God's essence.

Still, this attainment marks not the end but the beginning. A new life awaits the contemplative Christian with a structure of its own. Very little can be said about it—Ruusbroec's discussion of the God-seeing life is significantly brief—because we have moved into uncharted territory. Nevertheless, two points can and must be clarified. One is the lasting dialectic between contemplative and active life. The other concerns the relation between the one nature of God and the distinct modes of being of the three Persons. The two questions are connected, as we have already noted and as we shall see in more detail in the final chapter. In his conclusion of the God-seeking life, Ruusbroec defines the relation between the active and contemplative life in words that ought to be remembered throughout his discussion of the God-seeing stage. In the synopsis of chapter 65 he successively treats contemplation without intermediary and those periods of the contemplative life itself which are devoted to God-longing and the practice of virtue. Neither one of these discussions would be particularly new, were it not that they result in a synthesis of the two elements quite unique in mystical literature. In the discussion of the life in union when the inward man "has sunk himself in his essential being with the abysmal delights and riches of God" (II, 65), we are again struck by the negative quality of the early stage of unitive contemplation. Ruusbroec oddly combines the metaphor of darkness with that of light. "And from out the Divine Unity, there shines into him a simple light; and this light shows him Darkness and Nakedness and Nothingness" (ibid.). It is always hazardous to attach very specific meanings to the metaphorical language of a mystic. Yet Ruusbroec's customary precision here invites us to do so. Thus I would be inclined to interpret the passage as a trinitarian interpretation of the experience of negative theology. The light usually refers to the Son's revelation of the Father (as is clearly the case in the third book). Yet since we find ourselves at the beginning of contemplative life in the realm of the Father, that is, the realm of darkness and silence, all the Light reveals is precisely that darkness and nothingness. This remains by no means the case when we advance in contemplative life. Eventually Light (the Son) and Love (the Holy Spirit) will win out over darkness.

The specific character of the active life at this contemplative stage appears in Ruusbroec's presentation of virtue. Not the virtues of the novice, but those emerging from the "Savoring Wisdom, the ground and origin of all virtues" (II, 65). This gift of *recta sapere*, itself the basis of the contemplative life, suggests that passivity underlies even the active practice of the contemplative. The active life itself partakes in the passive contemplation. Still it remains a meeting with God "through an intermediary," a "way of longing" and "likeness" rather than of possession and identity.

Most remarkably, though, Ruusbroec adds a third way which combines action and fruition in such a manner "that the one never impedes, but always strengthens the other" (II, 65). Here rest and work alternate. For Ruusbroec, this mixture is the ideal of the true contemplative. Underneath this judgment we detect a solid acquaintance with human nature, which, even after having reached the highest peaks, is not capable of staying there all the time. Living occurs essentially in a rhythm of systole and diastole. Without this alternation the life energy becomes depleted. But the theological insight that the divine life itself, in which the contemplative is allowed to partake, consists of resting in unity and working in multiplicity plays an equally significant part in Ruusbroec's synthesis. Thus the "just" person who leads the "common life," "goes *toward* God with fervent love in eternal activity; and he goes *in* God with fruitive inclination in eternal rest" (II, 65).

·5·

From Trinity to Unity

Spiritual life consists in a process of unification: of the virtuous life in the heart, of the God-seeking life in the mind, of the God-seeing life in the spirit. It would be erroneous, however, to conceive of this unification as if it were a process of mental concentration. Each state of unity in spiritual life, especially the final one, requires God's direct intervention and hence is at least partly passive. The point where God and the soul touch lies beyond all active efforts. The soul contains the Image of God, or, more correctly, the soul is contained within that eternal Image which is God himself. Spiritual life, then, in the end consists in allowing oneself to enter that *superessence* of the soul, God's triune life. As we know, the highest union occurs in two different ways. Without intermediacy God unites the soul with himself, beyond all ideas, efforts, or virtues of its own, indeed, beyond created grace itself. This immediate union is always accompanied by one "with means," in which the soul, by the aid of created grace and the mostly passive use of its own powers, radiates this unity out over the multiplicity of creation.

Even in its expanding movement the soul remains under God's constant guidance, which eventually returns it to the unity without means. Ruusbroec is a realistic, practical master who never allows the spiritual aspirant to take off into mystical speculation without being moored in solid virtue. Nor does he allow the contemplative to "rest" without working. For him, being adopted into the life of the Trinity means moving into a storm, an active volcano. It includes moving "out" as much as moving "in," flowing forth into charity and good works, as much as withdrawing into solitary recollection.

In the third book of *The Spiritual Marriage*, Ruusbroec develops the final stage of the spiritual process in four short chapters. They deal with the paroxysm of the mystical consciousness. Yet their significance reaches beyond the strictly mystical realm. For the structure of the spiritual model here presented remains the same on all levels. Indeed, the mystical life does not consist in an abrupt alteration of consciousness, but rather in an evermore intensively conscious recurrence of the same divine rhythm. It is a rhythm of which every devout person has had at least some experience. What happens on the highest peaks of mystical life displays a genuine family resemblance with life in the spiritual valleys where most of us dwell. In the four chapters, then, of his third book, Ruusbroec attempts to draw a synthesis of the life in union, rather than a descriptive picture of its individual states or concepts.

In the first chapter Ruusbroec describes the "superessential" (*overweselijc*) contemplation, the one corresponding to the God-seeing life as such. Though it accompanies the *essential* union of the spirit with God,

Ruusbroec calls it *superessential*, because it totally transcends the natural powers of the soul and depends entirely on God's gratuitous communication. And yet to reach a superessential state of being is, in some sense, the vocation of all humans. What else is the *lumen gloriae* that enlightens the eternal beatitude? And the "uncreated grace" which theology calls the common share of the elect? The very existence of a superessential state confirms that the very essence of the self is determined by what surpasses it altogether—an idea which Kierkegaard once expressed as: If men forget to live religiously, they also forget to exist humanly. *Superessential* then refers to that aspect of my being in which I am most fully myself yet which I can never consider my own—because I share it with God. I am reminded of Gabriel Marcel's word: "The device of the person is not *sum* [as Descartes suggested], but *sursum*."

The fundamental character of the superessential union by no means implies, however, that all devout people reach it. "Few men can attain to this Divine seeing, because of their own incapacity and the mysteriousness of the light in which one sees" (III, 1). And even more emphatically: "Only he with whom it pleases God to be united in His Spirit, and whom it pleases Him to enlighten by Himself, can see God, and no one else" (III, 1).[1] In a sense the superessential contemplation

---

1. The words immediately preceding this quote have been mistranslated. The translation reads: "[T]he lover who is inward and righteous, him will it please God in His freedom to choose and to lift up into a superessential contemplation" (p. 167), but the orginal: "The lover who is inward and righteous *whom* it pleases God in his freedom . . ."—the restrictive "whom" has been omitted in English, thus converting a gratuitous choice into a necessary process.

began already with the "dark" contemplation which we have described in the preceding chapter. It also reflects the essential union. But the contemplation of darkness and nothingness merely initiated the superessential state. All of the third book shows how much more there is to divine contemplation than darkness. Ruusbroec refers to the state of "waylessness" as a precondition for the superessential contemplation: "Thirdly, he must have lost himself in a Waylessness and in a Darkness, in which all contemplative men wander in fruition and wherein they never again can find themselves in a creaturely way" (III, 1). There the spirit died to itself, here it comes to divine life.

The superessential contemplation is the state of consciousness that, to the full extent of its God-given ability, participates in the life of the Trinity. However much this state transcends the soul's natural powers, it never results in a pantheistic merger—a *hen kai pan*—but remains an encounter in love and hence preserves distinctness. Ruusbroec insists that the contemplative must "cleave to God with adhering intention and love" (III, 1). Contemplation is an ecstatic state that requires a "going out from ourselves" (III, 3). On the part of God, also, it is love that creates union. "All the riches which are in God by nature we possess by way of love in God, and God in us, through the unmeasured love which is the Holy Ghost" (III, 3). The contemplative's union with God consists entirely in being embraced by God. "In this embrace, in the essential unity of God, all inward spirits are one with God in the immersion of love" (III, 1). In God himself love achieves the essential unity of the Persons. "The mysterious Divine Nature is eternally and actively beholding and loving according to the Persons, and has everlasting fruition in a mutual embrace of the Persons in the unity of the Essence" (III, 1). The essential unity of the Persons in God's one nature *consists in* the mutual embrace of the Persons in love. For Ruusbroec there is no unity *beyond* the Trinity (as for Eckhart), not even a divine nature *beyond* the Persons. The unity of God's nature is the *same* divine love which expands into the distinctness of the Persons. That love (which is God himself) has two moments, a contracting (the one nature) and an expanding (the distinctness of the Persons). The superessential contemplation partakes in both movements: from the wayless darkness to the generation in love, and back into the unity of love. "But he who is united with God, and is enlightened in this truth, he is able to understand the truth by itself. For to comprehend and to understand God above all similitudes, such as He is in Himself, is to be God with God" (III, 1). This strong statement goes to the heart of the Christian mystery. It reasserts Athanasius' celebrated expression, God became man so that man might become God. To be God with God—that, according to Ruusbroec, is the very end of a Christian's spiritual life. We tend to qualify those words to the point where they become drained of meaning. But Christianity allows the faithful to believe that they can be with God without any intermediary other than God's own Word.

Nor is that divine life merely shrouded in darkness. "For our heavenly Father wills that we should see" (III, 1). True, there are no more ways or similitudes, no adequate words to describe the highest union. Yet the person elevated to this union becomes enlightened by the same light in which God sees himself. "[F]or He is the Father of Light, and this is why He utters eternally, without intermediary and without interruption, in the hiddenness of our spirit, one unique and abysmal word, and no other" (III, 1). That Word is the one he speaks uninterruptedly within himself. Here Ruusbroec decisively takes his distance from any terminally negative theology. The theology of darkness occupies a rightful place in Christian spiritual life as a preparatory moment. But it deviates from the Christian tradition when emphasized to the exclusion of divine illumination. There is no substitute for negation and self-denial, no spiritual life without tears. But to stay in the negation means to remain on the creaturely level and to refuse to follow when God invites us into his *own* light. For in himself God is not simply darkness or silence. His silence has brought forth the eternal Word; in his darkness shines the eternal Light. A permanently negative theology, then, rests upon a decision not to move beyond what I can see with my *own* eyes and hear with my *own* ears. It fails, by insufficiency, not because it negates, but because it negates too timidly. The devout Christian has to open his ears for God's own sound, his eyes for God's own light.

The negative expressions remain stark and strong in Ruusbroec's description of the superessential contemplation. "The spiritual man must have lost himself in a waylessness." The contemplative wanders around in an unknown land. He will never again find himself at home in the familiar world of predictable creatures. Nor can he ever again be satisfied with a created image of God. Those who have encountered God directly hold far fewer preconceived ideas about him than most of us. They are more willing to take risks and to consider unfamiliar, even daring theological positions. Regarding as presumptuous any claim about what God is supposed to do or to be, they are less shocked by novelty. In the uncharted territory of God's being, preconceptions are prejudices. Yet that does not mean that the spiritual person must remain in permanent darkness. "For in this darkness there shines and is born an incomprehensible Light, which is the Son of God, in Whom we behold eternal life. And in this light one becomes seeing" (III, 1). It is not that I see the light, but I become seeing in the light itself—the light is my seeing. As in Psalm 36, "In your light we see light." The spirit "is changed without interruption into that brightness which it receives" (III, 1). This light provides its own interpretation and justification, while the creatures remain dark and silent. "[H]ere there is nothing but an eternal seeing and staring at that Light, by that Light, and in that Light" (III, 2). It is in that Light that the Bridegroom comes.

In the second chapter Ruusbroec describes the rhythm of this divine coming, a coming that occurs "beyond time, in an eternal Now" (III, 2). How can there be rhythm "beyond time," motion in an eternal Now? Because the birth of the Son and His return to the Father occurs in the Now of eternity. Time for Aristotle is the essence of motion. But the theology of the Trinity introduces motion beyond time, difference without succession. The soul is called to participate in that timeless moment which is at the core of all creation. "[T]hrough the Eternal Birth, all creatures have come forth in eternity, before they were created in time" (III, 3).

In the third and fourth chapters, among the richest in all mystical literature, Ruusbroec describes this divine rhythm of contraction and expansion as the soul actively participates in it. The spirit's alternation from active out-going in virtue and charity to withdrawal into unmediated unity follows, in its own way, the internal divine motion from Trinity to Unity. The third chapter, taking its lead from the phrase of the Gospel pericope of the ten virgins, "Go ye out...", describes primarily the expanding, out-going movement. But since the elevation to superessential contemplation begins itself with a divine *embrace*, that is, a unifying contracting movement, Ruusbroec first describes that adoption into the unity of God's one nature. He reminds us how the contemplative life began: "[T]hrough this love we are dead to ourselves, and have gone forth in loving immersion into the Waylessness and Darkness" (III, 3). But this, however essential, remains preparatory to the encounter proper in light and in love. "There the spirit is embraced by the Holy Trinity, and dwells for ever within the superessential Unity, in rest and fruition. And in that same Unity, according to Its fruitfulness, the Father dwells in the Son, and the Son in the Father, and all creatures dwell in Both. And this is above the distinction of the Persons; for here by means of the reason we understand Fatherhood and Sonhood as the life-giving fruitfulness of the Divine Nature" (III, 3).

The divine unity, then, is in fact a dynamic union that eternally bursts out into an exodus and return. "Here there arise and begin an eternal going out and an eternal work which is without beginning; for here there is a beginning with beginning" (III, 3): in God there is no past or future. The divine operation is indeed the *beginning* of all that is, including his own being. It also constitutes the *permanent* foundation of all that exists within and outside God. Thus the God-seeing spirit is invited to witness the divine generation of the Son and, in him, as in their divine Archetype, the orgin of all created being. This trinitarian life knows no *past*. All occurs in an enduring *Now*. Even creation takes place in a divine present. "This eternal going out and this eternal life, which we have and are in God eternally, without ourselves, is the cause of our created being in time. And our created being abides in the Eternal Essence, and is one with its essential existence.... [T]his likeness is one with that same Image of the Holy Trinity, which is the wisdom of God and in which God beholds Himself and all things in an eternal Now, without before and after" (III, 3).

In our attempts to represent the beginning of creation, we usually think of the formation of the first stars. But the real wonder of the beginning lies in the aboriginal "resolution" of the Absolute to become manifest. In the eternal Now of the Father's Word, creation receives its primordial being, before and after its development in time. "So God has seen and known them in Himself, according to distinction, in living ideas, and in an otherness from Himself; but not as something other in all ways, for all that is in God is God" (III, 3). Nowhere does Ruusbroec claim that the creation and the birth of the Son coincide. In the Son God's selfhood becomes Image, while remaining God. In creation God's Image turns into otherness. But the creature is not "other" in all respects, for it remains *in* God. The eternal Word remains the immanent cause of its created being in time. "And our created being abides in the Eternal essence, and is one with it in its essential existence. And this eternal life and being, which we have and are in the eternal Wisdom of God, is like unto God" (III, 3). Moving into the otherness of creation the spiritual person still moves into an otherness that is grounded in God's eternal Image, and hence that retains God's presence and similitude. But only the spiritually pure are able to see this divine Image in creation. St. Francis, when looking at nature, literally *saw* it as an image of God. He saw creation with God's eyes, because he viewed it *from within* God. From that point of view "this likeness is one with that same Image of the Holy Trinity, which is the Wisdom of God and in which God beholds Himself and all things in an eternal Now." (III, 3) That likeness reflects a deeper identity of the creature with God's uncreated Image, an identity which only the spiritual person fully realizes.

In moving out into creation the contemplative merely follows God's own movement from hiddenness to manifestation. He partakes in God's exodus toward "otherness," toward that which depends on God through an intermediary. The contemplative makes this move *from within* the identity of God's trinitarian life. In this respect his attitude differs from that of the spiritual novice who, still intent upon the discovering of "likeness," looks for analogies and similitudes, and, in his own life, conformity through the practice of virtue. To the contemplative the move into creation forms an integral part of the mostly passive unification process itself. By the same token the spiritual person views that created multiplicity as being on its way back to God's unity. Not only does each creature return to its divine Image, but that Image itself returns to the unity of divine nature in its loving embrace of the Father.

Ruusbroec develops this return to unity, into God and within the Trinity, in the final chapter of *The Spiritual Marriage*, as a gloss upon the last words of the cry the ten virgins heard in the night: "[Go ye out] to meet Him." The "meeting" consists in a return to unity, a return that occurs under the impulses of the divine principle of personified Love, the Holy Spirit. "And that same Wisdom [the Son], with all that lives in It [creation], is actively turned back towards the Father, that is, towards that very ground from which It comes forth. And in this meeting, there comes forth the third Person, between the Father and the Son, that is, the Holy Ghost, Their mutual Love, who is one with them Both in the same nature" (III, 4). With the Son we reenter the living unity of that trinitarian embrace. Once again we find ourselves in the dark, for this contracting movement suspends all distinctions. "Now this active meeting and this loving embrace are in their ground fruitive and wayless; for the abysmal Waylessness of God is so dark and so unconditioned that it swallows up in itself every Divine way and activity, and all the attributes of the

Persons, within the rich compass of the essential Unity" (III, 4). But this wayless darkness differs from the *via negativa* with which the contemplative initiated the superessential union. For this is the love-night of the soul with God, "the dark silence in which all lovers lose themselves" (III, 4). The recurring rhythm of spiritual life is not a repetition; its ascending spiral never returns to the same point. With this return to divine unity *The Spiritual Marriage* concludes. But not the continuing alternation from being to work, from essence to manifestation.

Ruusbroec refers to this vital synthesis of an expanding and a contracting movement as "the common life" (*dat ghemeyne leven*). One of his richest concepts, it has also remained one of the hardest to define. The "common life" denotes at once the highest communion of the Persons in the one divine nature and the contemplative's total devotion both to God and to his creation. It presents that wonderful synthesis of the godly life which Christ incarnated in his terrestrial existence.

> He was sent down to earth to the common [*ghemeyne*] benefit of all men who would turn to Him.... Now mark how Christ gave Himself to all [*ghemeyne*] in perfect loyality. His inward and sublime prayer flowed forth towards His Father, and it was a prayer for all in common [*ghemeyne*] who desired to be saved. Christ was common to all [*ghemeyne*] in love, in teaching, in tender consolation, in generous gifts, in merciful forgiveness. His soul and His body, His life and His death and His ministry were, and are common to all [*ghemeyne*].
> (II, 45)

Any translation here fights a losing battle in attempting to render a newly coined term so comprehensive as to surpass any single English word. Nevertheless, from the quoted passage as well as from others (especially the famous portrait in *The Kingdom of the Lovers*) powerfully emerges the idea of a life that is the opposite of withdrawn, individualistic, or alien to this world—the negative qualities all too often associated with an intensive spiritual life. There is, as one commentator has observed, a certain greatness in a spiritual doctrine able to express its highest ideal in the most modest, simple, down-to-earth terms. Even greater is this doctrine for teaching that the summit of mystical contemplation, far from removing the contemplative from his fellow humans, leads him back to them to share their "common life." But greatest of all is it to assert this paradoxical ideal as the only possible and necessary one, because it follows the rhythm of God's own "common life."[2]

Trinitarian spirituality, however daring in its speculation, is never esoteric. It is an outgoing, creature-oriented form of contemplation that, following its divine exemplar, dares to move out into the world in the certainty that it will not move away from the divine unity. What links the most remote creature to the core of the godhead is love, love not as a subjective attitude, but love as the Person that God self is. In that Love the fragments of our world recombine and the pattern becomes visible, and the part returns to the whole.

---

2. Paul Henry, "La mystique trinitaire du bienheureux Jean Ruusbroec," *Recherches de Science Religieuse* 41 (1953): 74–75.

APPENDIX

The Spiritual Marriage
by Jan Ruusbroec

BOOK II

Chapter 56

Showing the way in which we shall meet God in a ghostly manner both with and without means (17)

Now I have shown you how the free and uplifted man becomes, through the grace of God, seeing in his inward practices. And we see that this is the first point which Christ demands and desires of us, where He says: BE-HOLD. As to the second and third points, wherein He says: THE BRIDEGROOM COMETH, and: GO YE OUT, I have shown you the three ways of the inward coming of Christ; and further that the first coming has four degrees, and how we are to go out with practices answering to each

Taken from John of Ruysbroeck, *The Adornment of the Spiritual Marriage, The Sparkling Stone, and The Book of Supreme Truth,* translated from the Flemish by Dom C. A. Wijnschenck (London, 1916).

way in which God inwardly enkindles, teaches, and moves us. Now we must consider the fourth point, which is the last. This is the meeting with Christ our Bridegroom. For all our inward and ghostly vision, in grace or in glory, and all our going out in the virtues, in whatsoever practices this be done, it is all for the sake of a meeting and a union with Christ our Bridegroom: for He is our eternal rest and the end and wage of all our labour.

You know that every meeting is a coming together of two persons, who come from different places, which are separated from, and opposite to, each other. Now Christ comes from above as a Lord and generous Giver, who can do all things. And we come from below as the poor servants, who can do nothing of ourselves, but have need of everything. The coming of Christ to us is from within outwards, and we go towards Him from without inwards; and this is why a ghostly meeting must here take place. And this coming and this meeting of ourselves and Christ takes place in two ways, to wit, with means and without means.

Chapter 57

Of the essential meeting with God without means in the nakedness of our nature

Now understand and mark this well. The unity of our spirit has two conditions: it is essential, and it is active. You must know that the spirit, according to its essence, receives the coming of Christ in the nakedness of its nature, without means and without interruption. For the being and the life which we are in God, in our Eternal Image, and which we have within ourselves according to our essence, this is without means and indivisible. And this is why the spirit, in its inmost and highest part, that is in its naked nature, receives without interruption the impress of its Eternal Archetype, and the Divine Brightness; and is an eternal dwelling-place of God in which God dwells as an eternal Presence, and which He visits perpetually, with new comings and with new instreamings of the ever-renewed brightness of His eternal birth. For where He comes, there He is; and where He is, there He comes. And where He has never been, thereto He shall never come; for neither chance nor change are in Him. And everything in which He is, is in Him; for He never goes out of Himself. And this is why the spirit in its essence possesses God in the nakedness of its nature, as God does the spirit: for it lives in God and God in it. And it is able, in its highest part to receive, without intermediary, the Brightness of God, and all that God can fulfil. And by means of the brightness of its Eternal Archetype, which shines in it essentially and personally, the spirit plunges itself and loses itself, as regards the highest part of its life (18), in the Divine Being, and there abidingly possesses its eternal blessedness; and it flows forth again, through the eternal birth of the Son, together with all the other creatures, and is set in its created being by the free will of the Holy Trinity. And here it is like unto the image of the most high Trinity in Unity, in which it has been made. And, in its created being, it incessantly receives the impress of its Eternal Archetype, like a flawless mirror, in which the image remains steadfast, and in which the reflection is renewed without interruption by its ever-new reception in new light. This essential union of our spirit with God does not exist in itself, but it dwells in God, and it flows forth from God, and it depends upon God, and it returns to God as to its Eternal Origin (19). And in this wise it has never been, nor ever shall be, separated from God; for this union is within us by our naked nature, and, were this nature to be separated from God, it would fall into pure nothingness. And this union is above time and space, and is always and incessantly active according to the way of God. But our nature, forasmuch as it is indeed like unto God but in itself is creature, receives the impress of its Eternal Image passively. This is that nobleness which we possess by nature in the essential unity of our spirit, where it is united with God according to nature. This neither makes us holy nor blessed, for all men, whether good or evil, possess it within themselves; but it is certainly the first cause of all holiness and all blessedness. This is the meeting and the union between God and our spirit in the nakedness of our nature.

Chapter 58

Showing how one is like unto God through grace and unlike unto God through mortal sin

Now consider this thought earnestly; for if you understand well that which I will now tell you, and that which

I have told you, you will have understood all the Divine truth which any creature can teach you, and far more besides. Otherwise does our spirit keep itself in that same unity when it is conceived as acting or working: for then it exists in itself as in its created and personal being. This is the source of the higher powers, and here there are beginning and end of all the creaturely works which are worked in a creaturely way, both in nature and above nature. Yet here the unity does not work forasmuch as it is unity; but all the powers of the soul in what way soever they work, derive their strength and their power from their proper source, that is, from the unity of the spirit, where it dwells in its personal being.

In this unity, the spirit must always either be like unto God through grace and virtue, or unlike unto God through mortal sin. For, that man has been made after the likeness of God, means that he has been created in the grace of God; the which grace is a God-formed light, which shines through us and makes us like to God; and without this light, which makes us God-like, we cannot be united with God supernaturally, even though we cannot lose the image of God nor our natural unity with Him (20). If we lose the likeness, that is, the grace of God, we are damned. And therefore, whenever God finds within us some capacity for the reception of His grace, it is His pleasure and His free goodness to make us, through His gifts, full of life, and like unto Him. This always happens whenever we turn to Him with our whole will; for at that very moment, Christ comes to us and in us, both with means and without means, that is, with the virtues and above the virtues. And He impresses His image and His likeness in us, namely Himself and His gifts: and He redeems us from sin, and makes us free and like unto Himself. And in that same working, through which God redeems us from sins, and makes us free and like unto Him through charity, the spirit immerses itself in fruitive love (21). And here there take place a meeting and a union which are without means and above nature, and wherein our highest blessedness consists. Although all that He gives us from love and free goodness is natural to God, for us, according to our condition, it is accidental and supernatural. For before, we were strangers and unlike unto God; and afterwards, becoming like Him, have received union with God.

Chapter 59

Showing how one possesses God in union and rest, above all likeness through grace

This meeting and this union, which the loving spirit achieves in God and possesses without means, must take place in the essential intuition, deeply hidden from our understanding; unless it be an effective understanding according to the way of simplicity (22). In the fruition of this unity we shall rest evermore, above ourselves and above all things. From this unity, all gifts, both natural and supernatural, flow forth, and yet the loving spirit rests in this unity above all gifts; and here there is nothing but God, and the spirit united with God without means. In this unity we are taken possession of by the Holy Ghost, and we take possession of the Holy Ghost and the Father and the Son, and the whole Divine Nature: for God cannot be divided. And the fruitive tendency of the spirit (23), which seeks rest in God above all likeness, receives and possesses in a supernatural way, in its essential being, all that the spirit ever received in a natural way. All good men experience this; but *how* it is, this remains hidden from them all their life long if they do not become inward and empty of all creatures. In that very moment in which man turns away from sin, he is received by God in the essential unity of his own being, at the summit of his spirit, that he may rest in God, now and evermore. And he also receives grace, and likeness unto God, in the proper source of his powers, that he may evermore grow and increase in new virtues. And as long as this likeness endures in charity and in virtues, so long also endures the union in rest. And this cannot be lost save only by mortal sin.

Chapter 60

Showing how we have need of the grace of God, which makes us like unto God and leads us to God without means

Now all holiness and all blessedness lie in this: that the spirit is led upwards, through likeness and by means of grace or glory, to rest in the essential unity. For the grace of God is the way by which we must always go, if we would enter into the naked essence in which God gives Himself with all His riches without means. And this is why the sinners and the damned spirits dwell in darkness; for they lack the grace of God, which should enlighten them, and lead them, and show them the way to the fruitive unity. Yet the essential being of the spirit is so noble, that even the damned cannot will their own annihilation. But sin builds up a barrier, and gives rise to such darkness and such unlikeness between the power and the essence in which God lives, that the spirit cannot be united with its proper essence; which would be its own and its essential rest, did sin not impede it. For whosoever lives without sin, he lives in likeness unto God, and in grace, and God is his own. And so we have need of grace, which casts out sin, and prepares the way, and makes our whole life fruitful. And this is why Christ always comes into us through means, that is, through grace and multifarious gifts; and we too go out towards Him through means, that is, through virtues and diverse practices. And the more inward gifts He gives and the more deeply He stirs us, the more inward and delightful are the workings of our spirit, as you have already heard in all the ways which have been shown forth before. And here there is a perpetual renewal; for God ever gives new gifts, and our spirit ever turns inward in such wise as it is invited and as is bestowed on it by God, and in that meeting it always receives a higher renewal. And thus one grows continually into a higher life. And this active meeting is altogether through means; for the gifts of God and our virtues and the activity of our spirit are the means. And these means are necessary for all men and all spirits: for, without the mediation of God's grace and a loving turning to Him in freedom, no creature shall ever be saved.

Chapter 64

Of the highest degree of the most interior life

Now understand this well: that measureless Splendour of God, which together with the incomprehensible brightness, is the cause of all gifts and of all virtues—that same Uncomprehensible Light transfigures the fruitive tendency of our spirit and penetrates it in a way that is wayless; that is, through the Uncomprehended Light. And in this light the spirit immerses itself in fruitive rest; for this rest is wayless and fathomless, and one can know of it in no other way than through itself—that is, through rest. For, could we know and comprehend it, it would fall into modes and measures; then it could not satisfy us, but rest would become an eternal restlessness. And for this reason, the simple, loving and immersed tendency of our spirit works within us a fruitive love; and this fruitive love is abysmal. And the abyss of God calls to the abyss; that is, of all those who are united with the Spirit of God in fruitive love. This inward call is an inundation of the essential brightness, and this essential brightness, enfolding us in an abysmal love, causes us to be lost to ourselves, and to flow forth from ourselves into the wild darkness of the Godhead. And, thus united without means, and made one with the Spirit of God, we can meet God through God, and everlastingly possess with Him and in Him our eternal bliss.

Chapter 65

Of three kinds of most inward practices

This most inward life is practiced in three ways.

At times, the inward man performs his introspection simply, according to the fruitive tendency, above all activity and above all virtues, through a simple inward gazing in the fruition of love. And here he meets God without intermediary. And from out the Divine Unity, there shines into him a simple light; and this light shows him Darkness and Nakedness and Nothingness (26). In the Darkness, he is enwrapped and falls into somewhat which is in no wise, even as one who has lost his way. In the Nakedness, he loses the perception and discernment of all things, and is transfigured and penetrated by a simple light. In the Nothingness, all his activity fails him; for he is vanquished by the working of God's abysmal love, and in the fruitive inclination of his spirit he vanquishes God, and becomes one spirit with him. And in this oneness with the Spirit of God, he enters into a fruitive tasting and possesses the Being of God. And he is filled, according to the measure in which he has sunk himself in his essential being, with the abysmal delights and riches of God. And from these riches an envelopment and a plenitude of sensible love flow forth into the unity of the higher powers. And from this plenitude of sensible love, a savoury and penetrating satisfaction flows forth into the heart and the bodily powers. And through this inflow the man becomes immovable within, and helpless as regards himself and all his works. And in the deeps of his ground he knows and feels nothing, in soul or in body, but a singular radiance with a sensible well-being and an all-pervading savour. This is the first way, and it is the way of emptiness; for it makes a man empty of all things, and lifts him up above activity and above all the virtues. And it unites the man with God, and brings about a firm perseverance in the most interior practices which he can cultivate. When, however, any restlessness, or working of the virutes, puts intermediaries, or images, between the inward man and the naked introversion which he desires, then he is hindered in this exercise; for this way consists in a going out, beyond all things, into the Emptiness. This is the first form of the most inward exercise.

• • •

At times such an inward man turns towards God with ardent desire and activity; that he may glorify and honour Him, and offer up and annihilate in the love of God, his selfhood and all that he is able to do. And here he meets God through an intermediary. This intermediary is the gift of Savouring Wisdom, the ground and origin of all virtues; which enkindles and moves all good men according to the measure of their love, and at times so greatly stirs and enkindles the inward man through love, that all the gifts of God, and all that God may give, except the gift of Himself, seem too little to him, and cannot satisfy him, but rather increase his impatience. For he has an inward perception or feeling in his ground; where all the virtues begin and end, where love dwells, and where with ardent desire he offers up all his virtues to God. And here the hunger and thirst of love become so great that he perpetually surrenders himself, and gives up his own works, and empties himself, and is noughted in love, for he is hungry and thirsty for the taste of God; and, at each irradiation of God (27), he is seized by God, and more than ever before is newly touched by love. Living he dies, and dying he lives again. And in this way the desirous hunger and thirst of love are renewed in him every hour.

This is the second way, which is the way of longing, in which love dwells in the Divine likeness, and longs and craves to unite itself with God. This way is more profitable and honourable to us than the first, for it is the source of the first; for none can enter into the rest which is above all works save the man who has loved love with desire and with activity. And this is why the grace of God and our active love must both go before and follow after; that is to say, they must be practised both before and after. For without acts of love we cannot merit anything, neither achieve God, nor keep the possession of that which we have acquired through the works of love. And for this reason no one who has power over himself, and can practise love, should be idle. When, however, a good man lingers in any gift of God, or any creature, he will be hindered in this most inward exercise; for this exercise is a hunger which nothing can still, save God alone.

• • •

From these two ways the third way arises; and this is an inward life according to justice. Now understand this: God comes to us without ceasing, both with means and without means, and demands of us both action and fruition, in such a way that the one never impedes, but always strengthens, the other. And therefore the most inward man lives his life in these two ways: namely, in work and in rest (28). And in each he is whole and undivided; for he is wholly in God because he rests in fruition, and he is wholly in himself because he loves in activity: and he is perpetually called and urged by God to renew both the rest and the work. And the justice of the spirit desires to pay every hour that which is demanded of it by God. And therefore, at each irradiation of God, the spirit turns inward, in action and in fruition; and thus it is renewed in every virtue, and is more deeply immersed in fruitive rest. For God gives, in one gift, Himself and His gifts; and the spirit gives, at each introversion, itself and all its works. For by means of the simple irradiation of God and the fruitive tendency and melting away of love, the spirit has been united with God, and is incessantly transported into rest. And through the gifts of Understanding and Savouring Wisdom, it is touched in an active way, and perpetually enlightened and enkindled in love. And there is shown and presented to it in the spirit all that one may desire. It is hungry and thirsty, for it beholds the food of the angels and the heavenly drink. It works diligently in love, for it beholds its rest. It is a pilgrim; and it sees its country. In love it strives for victory; for it sees its crown. Consolation, peace, joy, beauty and riches, and all that can delight it, are shown without measure in ghostly images to the reason which is enlightened in God. And through this showing and the touch of God, love remains active. For this just man has established a true life in the spirit, in rest and in work, which shall endure eternally; but, after this life, it shall be changed into a higher state. Thus the man is just; and he goes *towards* God with fervent love in eternal activity; and he goes *in* God with fruitive inclination in eternal rest. And he dwells in God, and yet goes forth towards all creatures in universal love, in virtue, and in justice. And this is the supreme summit of the inward life. All those men who do not possess both rest and work in one and the same exercise, have not yet attained this justice. This just man cannot be hindered in his introversion, for he turns inward both in fruition and in work; but he is like to a double mirror, which receives images on both sides. For in his higher part, the man receives God with all His gifts; and, in his lower part, he receives bodily images through the senses. Now he can enter into himself at will, and can practise justice without hindrance. But man is unstable in this life, and that is why he often turns outwards, and works in the senses, without need and without the command of the enlightened reason; and thus he falls into venial sins. But in the loving introversion of the just man all venial sins are like to drops of water in a glowing furnace.

And with this I leave the inward life.

BOOK III

Chapter 1

Showing the three ways by which one enters into the God-seeing life

The inward lover of God, who possesses God in fruitive love, and himself in adhering and active love, and his whole life in virtues according to righteousness; through these three things, and by the mysterious revelation of God, such an inward man enters into the God-seeing life. Yea, the lover who is inward and righteous, him will it please God in His freedom to choose and to lift up into a superessential contemplation, in the Divine Light and according to the Divine Way (32). This contemplation sets us in purity and clearness above all our understanding, for it is a singular adornment and a heavenly crown, and besides the eternal reward of all virtues and of our whole life. And to it none can attain through knowledge and subtlety, neither through any exercise whatsoever. Only he with whom it pleases God to be united in His Spirit, and whom it pleases Him to enlighten by Himself, can see God, and no one else. The mysterious Divine Nature is eternally and actively beholding and loving according to the Persons, and has everlasting fruition in a mutual embrace of the Persons in the unity of the Essence. In this embrace, in the essential Unity of God, all inward spirits are one with God in the immersion of love; and are that same one which the Essence is in Itself, according to the mode of Eternal Bliss (33). And in this most high unity of the Divine Nature, the heavenly Father is origin and beginning of every work which is worked in heaven and on earth. And He says in the deep-sunken hiddenness of the spirit: BEHOLD, THE BRIDEGROOM COMETH; GO YE OUT TO MEET HIM.

These words we will now explain and set forth in their relation to that superessential contemplation which is the source of all holiness, and of all perfection of life to which one may attain. Few men can attain to this Divine seeing, because of their own incapacity and the mysteriousness of the light in which one sees. And therefore no one will thoroughly understand the meaning of it by any learning or subtle consideration of his own; for all words, and all that may be learnt and understood in a creaturely way, are foreign to, and far below, the truth which I mean. But he who is united with God, and is enlightened in this truth, he is able to understand the truth by itself. For to comprehend and to understand God above all similitudes, such as He is in Himself, is to be God with God, without intermediary, and without any otherness that can become a hindrance or an intermediary. And therefore I beg every one who cannot understand this, or feel it in the fruitive unity of his spirit, that he be not offended at it, and leave it for that which it is: for that which I am going to say is true, and Christ, the Eternal Truth, has said it Himself in His teaching in many places, if we could but show and explain it rightly. And therefore, whosoever wishes to understand this must have died to himself, and must live in God, and must turn his gaze to the eternal light in the ground of his spirit, where the Hidden Truth reveals Itself without means. For our Heavenly Father wills that we should see; for He is the Father of Light, and this is why He utters eternally, without intermediary and without interruption, in the hiddenness of our spirit, one unique and abysmal word, and no other. And in this word, He utters Himself and all things. And this word is none other than: BEHOLD. And this is the coming forth and the birth of the Son of Eternal Light, in Whom all blessedness is known and seen.

• • •

Now if the spirit would see God with God in this Divine light without means, there needs must be on the part of man three things.

The first is that he must be perfectly ordered from without in all the virtues, and within must be unencumbered, and as empty of every outward work as if he did not work at all: for if his emptiness is troubled within by some work of virtue, he has an image; and as long as this endures within him, he cannot contemplate.

Secondly, he must inwardly cleave to God, with adhering intention and love, even as a burning and glowing fire which can never more be quenched. As long as he feels himself to be in this state, he is able to contemplate.

Thirdly, he must have lost himself in a Waylessness and in a Darkness, in which all contemplative men wander in fruition and wherein they never again can find themselves in a creaturely way. In the abyss of this darkness, in which the loving spirit has died to itself, there begin the manifestation of God and eternal life. For in this darkness there shines and is born an incomprehensible Light, which is the Son of God, in Whom we behold eternal life. And in this Light one becomes seeing; and this Divine Light is given to the simple sight of the spirit, where the spirit receives the brightness which is God Himself, above all gifts and every creaturely activity, in the idle emptiness in which the spirit has lost itself through fruitive love, and where it receives without means the brightness of God, and is changed without interruption into that brightness which it receives. Behold, this mysterious brightness, in which one sees everything that one can desire according to the emptiness of the spirit: this brightness is so great that the loving contemplative, in his ground wherein he rests, sees and feels nothing but an incomprehensible Light; and through that Simple Nudity which enfolds all things, he finds himself, and feels himself, to be that same Light by which he sees, and nothing else (34). And this is the first condition by which one becomes seeing in the Divine Light. Blessed are the eyes which are thus seeing, for they possess eternal life.

Chapter 2

How the eternal birth of God is renewed without interruption in the nobility of the spirit

When we have thus become seeing, we can behold in joy the eternal coming of our Bridegroom; and that is the second point of which we would speak. What is this coming of our Bridegroom which is eternal? It is the new birth and a new enlightenment without interruption; for the ground from which the Light shines forth, and which is the Light itself, is life-giving and fruitful, and therefore the manifestation of the Eternal Light is renewed without ceasing in the hiddenness of the spirit. Behold, every creaturely work, and every exercise of virtue, must here cease; for here God works alone in the high nobility of the spirit. And here there is nothing but an eternal seeing and staring at that Light, by that Light, and in that Light. And the coming of the Bridegroom is so swift that He is perpetually coming, and yet dwelling within with unfathomable riches; and ever coming anew, in His Person, without interruption, with such new brightness that it seems as though he had never come before. For His coming consists, beyond time, in an eternal NOW, which is ever received with new longings and new joy. Behold, the delight and the joy which this Bridegroom brings with Him in His coming are boundless and without measure, for they are Himself. And this is why the eyes with which the spirit sees and gazes at its Bridegroom, have opened so wide that they can never close again. For the spirit continues for ever to see and to stare at the secret manifestation of God. And the grasp of the spirit is opened so wide for the coming in of the Bridegroom, that the spirit itself becomes that Breadth Which it grasps. And so God is grasped and beheld through God; wherein rests all our blessedness. This is the second point: in which we receive, without interruption, the eternal coming of our Bridegroom in our spirit.

Chapter 3

How our spirit is called to go out in contemplation and fruition

Now the Spirit of God says in the secret outpouring of our spirit: Go YE OUT, in an eternal contemplation and fruition, according to the way of God. All the riches which are in God by nature we possess by way of love in God, and God in us, through the unmeasured love which is the Holy Ghost; for in this love one tastes of all that one can desire. And therefore through this love we are dead to ourselves, and have gone forth in loving immersion into Waylessness and Darkness. There the spirit is embraced by the Holy Trinity, and dwells for ever within the superessential Unity, in rest and fruition. And in that same Unity, according to Its fruitfulness, the Father dwells in the Son, and the Son in the Father, and all creatures dwell in Both. And this is above the distinction of the Persons; for here by means of the reason we understand Fatherhood and Sonhood as the life-giving fruitfulness of the Divine Nature.

Here there arise and begin an eternal going out and an eternal work which is without beginning; for here there is a beginning with beginning. For, after the Almighty Father had perfectly comprehended Himself in the ground of His fruitfulness, so the Son, the Eternal Word of the Father, came forth as the second Person in the Godhead. And, through the Eternal Birth, all creatures have come forth in eternity, before they were created in time. So God has seen and known them in Himself, according to distinction, in living ideas (35), and in an otherness from Himself; but not as something other in all ways, for all that is in God is God (36). This eternal going out and this eternal life, which we have and are in God eternally, without ourselves, is the cause of our created being in time. And our created being abides in the Eternal Essence, and is one with it in its essential existence. And this eternal life and being, which we have and are in the eternal Wisdom of God, is like unto God. For it has an eternal immanence in the Divine Essence, without distinction; and through the birth of the Son it has an eternal outflowing in a distinction and otherness, according to the Eternal Idea. And through these two points it is so like unto God that He knows and reflects Himself in this likeness without cessation, according to the Essence and according to the Persons. For, though even here there are distinction and otherness according to intellectual perception, yet this likeness is one with that same Image of the Holy Trinity, which is the wisdom of God and in which God beholds Himself and all things in an eternal Now, without before and after. In a single seeing He beholds Himself and all things. And this is the Image and the Likeness of God, and our Image and our Likeness; for in it God reflects Himself and all things. In this Divine Image all creatures have an eternal life, outside themselves, as in their eternal Archetype; and after this eternal Image, and in this Likeness, we have been made by the Holy Trinity. And therefore God wills that we shall go forth from ourselves in this Divine Light, and shall reunite ourselves in a supernatural way with this Image, which is our proper life, and shall possess it with Him, in action and in fruition, in eternal bliss.

For we know well that the bosom of the Father is our ground and origin, in which we begin our being and our life. And from our proper ground, that is from the Father and from all that lives in Him, there shines forth an eternal brightness, which is the birth of the Son. And in this brightness, that is, in the Son, the Father knows Himself and all that lives in Him; for all that He has, and all that He is, He gives to the Son, save only the property of Fatherhood, which abides in Himself. And this is why all that lives in the Father, unmanifested in the Unity, is also in the Son actively poured forth into manifestation: and the simple ground of our Eternal Image ever remains in darkness and in waylessness, but the brightness without limit which streams forth from it, this reveals and brings forth within the Conditioned the hiddenness of God. And all those men who are raised up above their created being into a God-seeing life are one with this Divine brightness. And they are that brightness itself, and they see, feel, and find, even by means of this Divine Light, that, as regards their uncreated essence, they are that same onefold ground from which the brightness without limit shines forth in the Divine way, and which, according to the simplicity of the Essence, abides eternally onefold and wayless within. And this is why inward and God-seeing men will go out in the way of contemplation, above reason and above distinction and above their created being, through an eternal intuitive gazing. By means of this inborn light they are transfigured, and made one with that same light through which they see and which they see (37). And thus the God-seeing men follow after their Eternal Image, after which they have been made; and they behold God and all things, without distinction, in a simple seeing, in the Divine brightness. And this is the most noble and the most profitable contemplation to which one can attain in this life; for in this contemplation, a man best remains master of himself and free. And at each loving introversion he may grow in nobility of life beyond anything that we are able to understand; for he remains free and master of himself in inwardness and virtue. And this gazing at the Divine Light holds him up above all inwardness and all virtue and all merit, for it is the crown and the reward after which we strive, and which we have and possess now in this wise; for a God-seeing life is a heavenly life. But were we set free from this misery and this exile, so we should have, as regards our created being, a greater capacity to receive this brightness; and so the glory of God would shine through us in every way better and more nobly. This is the way above all ways, in which one goes out through Divine contemplation and an eternal intuitive gazing, and in which one is transfigured and transmuted in the Divine brightness. This going out of the God-seeing man is also in love; for through the fruition of love he rises above his created being, and finds and tastes the riches and the delights which are God Himself, and which He causes to pour forth without interruption in the hiddenness of the spirit, where the spirit is like unto the nobility of God.

Chapter 4

Of a divine meeting which takes place in the hiddenness of our spirit

When the inward and God-seeing man has thus attained to his Eternal Image, and in this clearness, through the Son, has entered into the bosom of the Father: then he is enlightened by Divine truth, and he receives anew, every moment, the Eternal Birth, and he goes forth according to the way of the light, in a Divine contemplation. And here there begins the fourth and last point; namely, a loving meeting, in which, above all else, our highest blessedness consists.

You should know that the heavenly Father, as a living ground, with all that lives in Him, is actively turned towards His Son, as to His own Eternal Wisdom. And that same Wisdom, with all that lives in It, is actively turned back towards the Father, that is, towards that very ground from which It comes forth. And in this meeting, there comes forth the third Person, between the Father and the Son; that is the Holy Ghost, Their mutual Love, who is one with them Both in the same nature. And He enfolds and drenches through both in action and fruition the Father and the Son, and all that lives in Both, with such great riches and such joy that as to this all creatures must eternally be silent; for the incomprehensible wonder of this love, eternally transcends the understanding of all creatures. But where this wonder is understood and tasted without amazement (38), there the spirit dwells above itself, and is one with the Spirit of God; and tastes and sees without measure, even as God, the riches which are the spirit itself in the unity of the living ground, where it possesses itself according to the way of its uncreated essence.

Now this rapturous meeting is incessantly and actively renewed in us, according to the way of God; for the Father gives Himself in the Son, and the Son gives Himself in the Father, in an eternal content and a loving embrace; and this renews itself every moment within the bonds of love. For like as the Father incessantly beholds all things in the birth of His Son, so all things are loved anew by the Father and the Son in the outpouring of the

Holy Ghost. And this is the active meeting of the Father and of the Son, in which we are lovingly embraced by the Holy Ghost in eternal love.

Now this active meeting and this loving embrace are in their ground fruitive and wayless; for the abysmal Waylessness of God is so dark and so unconditioned that it swallows up in itself every Divine way and activity, and all the attributes of the Persons, within the rich compass of the essential Unity; and it brings about a Divine fruition in the abyss of the Ineffable. And here there is a death in fruition, and a melting and dying into the Essential Nudity, where all the Divine names, and all conditions, and all the living images which are reflected in the mirror of Divine Truth, lapse in the Onefold and Ineffable, in waylessness and without reason. For in this unfathomable abyss of the Simplicity, all things are wrapped in fruitive bliss; and the abyss itself may not be comprehended, unless by the Essential Unity. To this the Persons, and all that lives in God, must give place; for here there is nought else but an eternal rest in the fruitive embrace of an outpouring Love. And this is that wayless being which all interior spirits have chosen above all other things. This is the dark silence in which all lovers lose themselves. But if we would prepare ourselves for it by means of the virtues, we should strip ourselves of all but our very bodies, and should flee forth into the wild Sea, whence no created thing can draw us back again (39).

May we possess in fruition the essential Unity, and clearly behold unity in the Trinity; this may Divine Love, which turns no beggar away, bestow upon us. AMEN.

GENERAL THEOLOGICAL SEMINARY
NEW YORK